Inside Eye™

SPACE
AND OTHER FLYING
MACHINES

D0294079

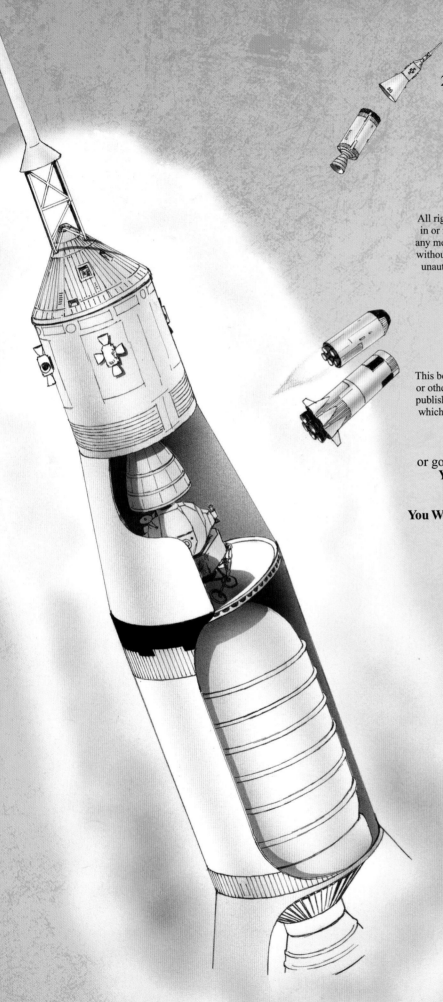

Published in Great Britain in MMXIV by
Book House, an imprint of
The Salariya Book Company Ltd
25 Marlborough Place, Brighton BN1 1UB
www.salariya.com
www.book-house.co.uk

PB ISBN-13: 978-1-909645-75-2

S A L A R I Y A

1 3 5 7 9 8 6 4 2

A CIP catalogue record for this book is available
from the British Library.

Printed and bound in China.

Visit our website at **www.book-house.co.uk**
or go to **www.salariya.com** for **free** electronic versions of:
You Wouldn't Want to be an Egyptian Mummy!
You Wouldn't Want to be a Roman Gladiator!
You Wouldn't Want to be a Polar Explorer!
You Wouldn't Want to sail on a 19th-Century Whaling Ship!

Visit
www.salariya.com
for our online catalogue and **free**
interactive web books.

PAPER FROM
SUSTAINABLE
FORESTS

Inside Eye™

SPACE
AND OTHER FLYING
MACHINES

Written by Margot Channing

CONTENTS

Into the Air

For thousands of years, people dreamed of being able to fly. Eventually, in 1903, the Wright brothers succeeded, with the first successful powered flight. In just over 100 years, even bigger and more sophisticated aircraft have taken to the skies to carry people and goods to every corner of the Earth.

This is an artist's impression of the *Graf Zeppelin*, one of the most extraordinary air machines of all time.

Conquering Space

Some remarkably powerful and complex craft have even left this planet to explore what lies beyond, in space. It began in 1957, when the Soviet Union launched *Sputnik 1*, the world's first artificial satellite, to orbit the Earth. Then, in 1969, on the *Apollo* 11 mission, US astronaut Neil Armstrong became the first human to set foot on the Moon. How long will it be before we travel to Mars?

The space shuttle is one of the most revolutionary vehicles of all time, making it possible for man to leave Earth and enter the wilderness of space.

The Boeing 747 is one of the largest and most famous of all passenger aeroplanes.

Inside Eye

In this book, we will look at incredible air and space machines to discover how they worked, how they were built, what they achieved and much more. And with an amazing 'inside eye' and stunning cutaway illustrations, we will show you exactly what each machine looks like – from the inside out.

The Great Airships

Airships were the giants of the sky. The two biggest were the *Graf Zeppelin* – 236 m long – and the *Hindenburg*, which, at 245 m, was longer than three jumbo jets placed end to end. Construction of the *Hindenburg* began in 1934 in Germany and it made its first flight in March 1936.

The gasbags in the *Hindenburg* airship were made from 1.5 million ox bladders.

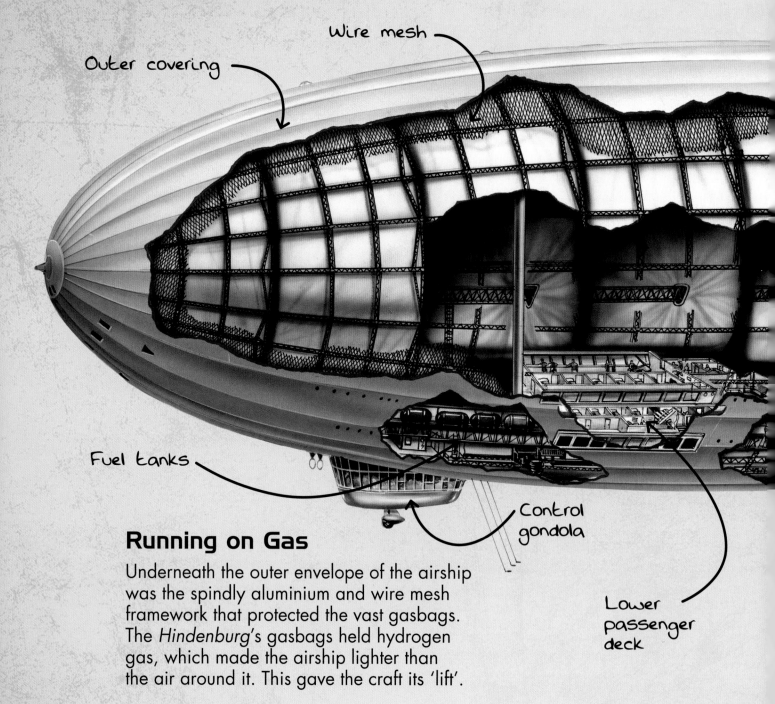

Wire mesh

Outer covering

Fuel tanks

Control gondola

Lower passenger deck

Running on Gas

Underneath the outer envelope of the airship was the spindly aluminium and wire mesh framework that protected the vast gasbags. The *Hindenburg*'s gasbags held hydrogen gas, which made the airship lighter than the air around it. This gave the craft its 'lift'.

Outside and Inside

The *Hindenburg*'s control gondola and its four engines each contained pods called nacelles. They were the only parts of the airship to break its streamlined shape. The passenger accommodation, which included cabins, a dining room, a reading and writing room, and a lounge, was inside the hull.

The control gondola of the *Graf Zeppelin* contained the control deck and crew's sleeping quarters.

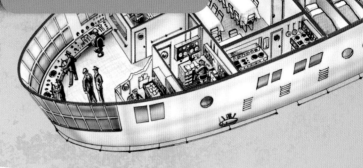

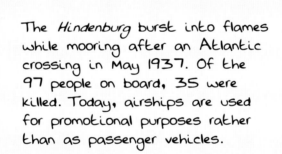

The *Hindenburg* burst into flames while mooring after an Atlantic crossing in May 1937. Of the 97 people on board, 35 were killed. Today, airships are used for promotional purposes rather than as passenger vehicles.

Nacelles

Living the High Life

Although it was expensive, and only 75 passengers could be carried on each trip, travel by airship became fashionable in the 1930s. Those passengers could cross the Atlantic Ocean in style in just over two days – half the time it took in a liner.

Empire Boats

Flying boats – aircraft that can take off from water and land on it – were widely used during the 1920s and 1930s. Airlines believed them to be safer than the aircraft usually used for long-distance sea and ocean crossings. The use of flying boats declined after World War II because thousands of concrete runways had been built and many long-range aircraft were developed during the conflict.

Post and Passengers

In 1934, the British government announced that an air-mail service would begin on routes to countries in the British Empire, such as South Africa and India. The British airline, Imperial Airways, ordered 28 new Short S23 C-class flying boats, which became known as 'Empire Boats.' The first was launched on July 2, 1936.

Baggage and mail hold

G-

Wartime Duties

The *Short Sunderland* was based on the Short C-class flying boat. It carried out a variety of wartime jobs, including anti-submarine warfare.

Long-distance Travel

The Empire Air Mail service began in June 1937. The first flight was made between Imperial Airways' new flying-boat base near Southampton, England, and Durban, South Africa. The service was extended to more destinations, and by June 1938, the Empire Boats were flying to Australia and New Zealand, and on to the Pacific Islands.

Passengers travelled in great comfort in luxurious cabins. High-quality meals were freshly cooked and served by a steward. Aeroplane service today is very different. Meals are prepared in bulk by companies on the ground and delivered to the aeroplane to be served during flights.

Flight deck

After landing, the flying boat was moored like a ship. Passengers boarded from the shore by motor launch.

Kitchen

Multimillionaire Howard Hughes (right) built the largest flying boat ever – the *Hughes H4 Spruce Goose*. Its wingspan of 97.5 m is the longest of any aircraft ever built.

Boeing 747

The Boeing 747 jumbo jet is one of the largest and most successful airliners ever designed. It first flew on 9 February 1969, and made its maiden commercial flight from New York to London in the colours of the US airline, Pan Am.

The Boeing 747-200 is 70.66 m long from nose to tail fin and has a 59.64 m wingspan. Its overall height is 19.33 m.

Long Service

The 747 is the workhorse of long-haul flying. Around 1,500 have been built and millions of people have flown in them. There are various versions of the aircraft, including the 747-200, shown here, and the 747-400, which is the most common version in service. The latest variation, the 747-8I, can carry up to 467 passengers and all their luggage. It also carries the food and fuel for the flight, flight crew and cabin staff.

Flight deck

Baggage hold

Heavy Lifting

Specially converted 747s are used to carry huge amounts of freight around the globe. There are around 300 aircraft in service, carrying half the world's air freight cargo.

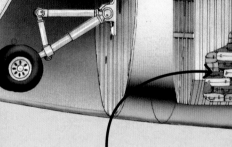

Safe and Easy

Despite its immense size, the Boeing 747 has a reputation among airline pilots as being easy to fly and has a good safety record. The fuselage is built from aluminium alloy, which is much lighter than steel. The engines are contained in pods attached to the wings with pylons, which are designed to break off if an engine seizes up.

Air conditioning ducts

Upper passenger deck

Lower passenger deck

The pilot of a 747 has to watch a huge number of instruments that give constant information about the flight.

Apollo 11

In 1961, President John F. Kennedy launched the North American Space Agency's (NASA) Moon-shot programme, stating that the nation's aim, before the decade was out, should be 'landing a man on the Moon and returning him safely to Earth.' In 1961, the United States had not yet put a person into orbit round Earth, so the president's goal seemed far-fetched to some.

Service module

Building a Spacecraft

A new type of space vehicle would be required to make the long trip to the Moon, land on it, and return to Earth. This vehicle was *Apollo*. The machine consisted of three sections: the command module, the service module and the lunar module. *Apollo* would carry three astronauts, two of whom would land on the Moon.

Apollo 11 was the first space machine to travel to the Moon.

Eagle Symbol

Apollo 11's badge showed an eagle, the national bird of the United States. *Eagle* was also the name of the lunar module.

APOLLO 11

Early Experiments

NASA carried out a series of missions in the early 1960s – in the *Mercury* and *Gemini* spacecraft. The voyages taught NASA the necessary skills to complete a trip to the Moon, which would require several dockings and perfect rocket firings.

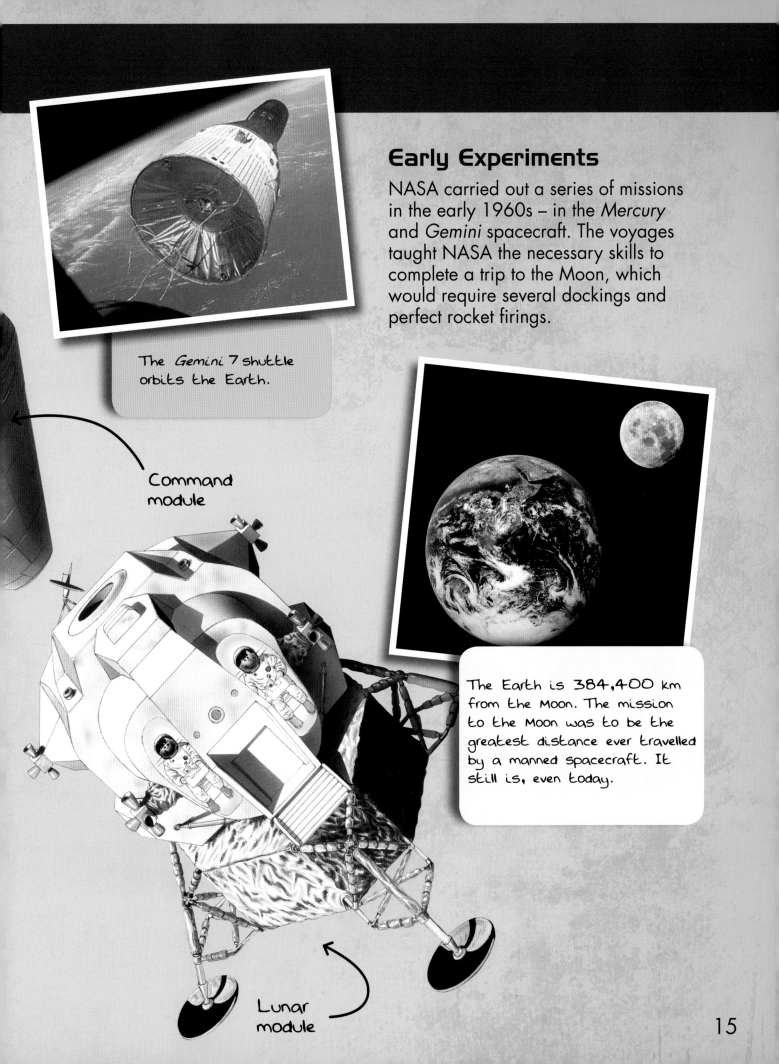

The *Gemini 7* shuttle orbits the Earth.

Command module

Lunar module

The Earth is 384,400 km from the Moon. The mission to the Moon was to be the greatest distance ever travelled by a manned spacecraft. It still is, even today.

The Mission

A series of *Apollo* missions were put in place to test the new spacecraft. Each would go one step further towards the ultimate goal. *Apollo* 5 and 6 went into space unmanned. *Apollo* 7 took astronauts into Earth's orbit. *Apollo* 8 took them into lunar orbit. The lunar module of *Apollo* was tested in missions 9 and 10.

Keeping the Promise

On 20 July 1969, the lunar module of *Apollo* 11 touched down on the Moon. Nearly six hours later, Neil Armstrong stepped onto the lunar surface. There were still five months left of the 1960s, so President Kennedy's promise of putting a man on the Moon within the decade had been fulfilled.

When the crew of *Apollo* 11 landed on the Moon, they accomplished what had once been thought impossible. Man's landing on the Moon marked the beginning of a new space age.

Neil Armstrong

The most famous of the three *Apollo* 11 astronauts was Neil Armstrong. He was the first man to walk on the Moon. Armstrong got his pilot's licence on his sixteenth birthday, flew for the US Navy and was a NASA test pilot.

Neil Armstrong

Edwin 'Buzz' Aldrin

The crew of *Apollo 11* are still famous around the world today for their daring space expedition.

Michael Collins

Apollo Crew

Edwin 'Buzz' Aldrin stepped onto the Moon a few minutes after Armstrong. Aldrin was an expert on docking spacecraft in orbit. Michael Collins was the third member of the crew. He kept the command module in orbit while the other two astronauts landed on the Moon. Collins was a former Air Force test pilot.

News of the historic Moon landing made headlines around the world. Today, Buzz Aldrin and Neil Armstrong are remembered as the first great space pioneers. Here, they are shown as waxwork models at Madame Tussauds in Washington, D.C.

17

Getting to the Moon

The *Apollo* 11 mission in 1969, and the five Moon landings that followed were extremely complicated operations. They needed a series of delicate spacecraft manoeuvres and dockings to work perfectly. As well as a new spacecraft, the Moon landing programme needed a rocket with much more lifting power than any yet in existence.

First-stage separation

Lunar module

Mighty Missile

In 1961, NASA began work on the *Saturn V* rocket, and first tested it in 1967. It was a three-stage rocket. It weighed nearly 2,700 tonnes (including its fuel), was 111 m high and could carry 136 tonnes of equipment into space.

Each of the three stages, or sections, lifted the *Apollo* spacecraft further into space.

Into Orbit

The *Saturn V* rocket orbited the Moon one and a half times. The command and service modules then detached from the lunar module, which began to turn in preparation to land on the Moon. The command and service modules stayed in orbit.

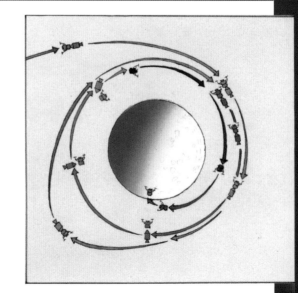

Three Stages

After lift-off, at a height of 65 km, the main engines shut down and the first stage separated. The second-stage engines took the rocket to 185 km above Earth. The third-stage rocket fired *Apollo* out of Earth's orbit towards the Moon and into the Moon's orbit.

Second-stage separation

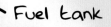

Fuel tank

An enormous amount of energy is required to launch a rocket from Earth into space. The first stage of the *Saturn V* rocket had five engines, each of which burned 3 tonnes of kerosene and liquid oxygen every second.

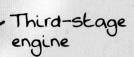

Third-stage engine

The *Apollo* 11 astronauts were on the Moon for only 22 hours. During that time, Armstrong and Aldrin set up a TV camera, gathered rock samples and raised the American flag, complete with a wire insert to hold it out because there is no wind on the Moon. They also set up several experiments, including a seismic unit to record lunar 'earthquakes'.

The two-seater LRV was powered by a small electric motor in each wheel, fed from batteries. The maximum speed was 16 kph, and battery life was 78 hours.

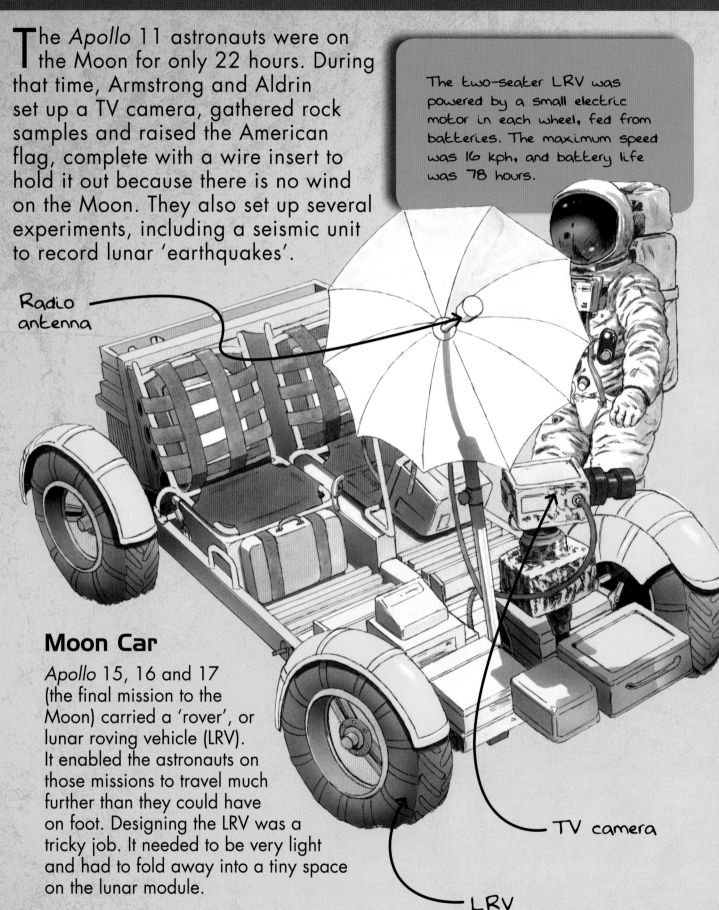

Radio antenna

TV camera

LRV

Moon Car

Apollo 15, 16 and 17 (the final mission to the Moon) carried a 'rover', or lunar roving vehicle (LRV). It enabled the astronauts on those missions to travel much further than they could have on foot. Designing the LRV was a tricky job. It needed to be very light and had to fold away into a tiny space on the lunar module.

Men at Work

The astronauts wore backpacks, known as portable life-support systems (PLSS), which kept them cool and carried their oxygen supply. Among the items left on the Moon by the *Apollo* 11 mission was a plaque signed by US President Richard Nixon and the three astronauts.

Foil collector

A foil collector on the lunar module caught minute particles from the Sun for later analysis.

10c
AIRMAIL

L_DAY U
FREEDOM UNDER THE

FIRST MAN ON THE MOON

UNITED STATES

Hundreds of millions of people watched live TV as Neil Armstrong, and later his colleague Buzz Aldrin, stepped onto the Moon. The event was marked with a series of celebrations and recorded in merchandising and memorabilia, including stamps.

Small Steps

The astronauts' boots left footprints in the lunar dust, which Armstrong described as fine and powdery.

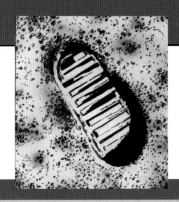

Return from the Moon

After 22 hours, the two *Apollo* 11 astronauts returned to the lunar module. They fired the engines on the ascent section and blasted off from the Moon's surface. Lift-off was smooth and they re-entered lunar orbit. The lunar module docked with the command and service modules, Armstrong and Aldrin rejoined Collins and the lunar module was jettisoned.

Parachute carries command module to Earth

Into the Ocean

The command module was the only part of the original *Saturn V* rocket to return to Earth. The mission had lasted for 195 hours and the astronauts had travelled more than 1.5 million km. After re-entry into Earth's atmosphere, the command module parachuted into the Pacific Ocean.

The astronauts splashed down into the ocean only about 36 minutes behind schedule.

Helicopter picks up the astronauts and carries them to the USS *Hornet*

Command module lands in the Pacific Ocean

Once the two astronauts had safely returned to the command module, the lunar module was then detached. It entered the Moon's orbit and then crashed into its surface.

Sea Rescue

A helicopter picked up the astronauts, who were then taken to the US Navy ship *USS Hornet*. They spent 18 days in quarantine before scientists confirmed that the Moon rock samples they had brought back contained no harmful micro-organisms.

On landing in the Pacific Ocean, the battered command module showed the marks of its hazardous journey. Thankfully, the module and its crew had survived the re-entry into the Earth's atmosphere.

Precious Cargo

When Armstrong and Aldrin left the Moon in the lunar module, they were carrying 21.5 kg of Moon rock and dust. They left important scientific experiments in place behind them.

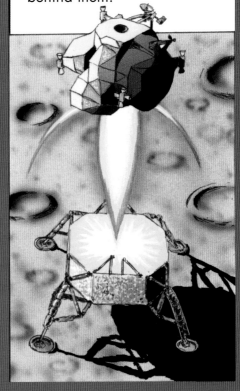

The Space Shuttle

The space shuttle, the world's first reusable spacecraft, was developed in the United States. The shuttle was part spacecraft, part aircraft and usually carried between four and seven astronauts. It launched like a rocket, orbited in space during its mission and glided back to Earth. The first space shuttle mission took place in 1981, and the last in 2011.

This shuttle is carrying *Spacelab*, the space laboratory of the European Space Agency (ESA), together with experimental equipment, monitored by the *Spacelab* scientists.

Experimental equipment

Space Workhorse

The five US space shuttles were *Atlantis, Columbia, Challenger, Discovery* and *Endeavour*. They deployed and recovered satellites, carried scientific experiments into space and performed top-secret military missions. Each shuttle was 37 m long, with a wingspan of 25 m. The payload bay was 18.3 m long and could carry up to 29.5 tonnes of cargo.

Cutaway of nose section of space shuttle

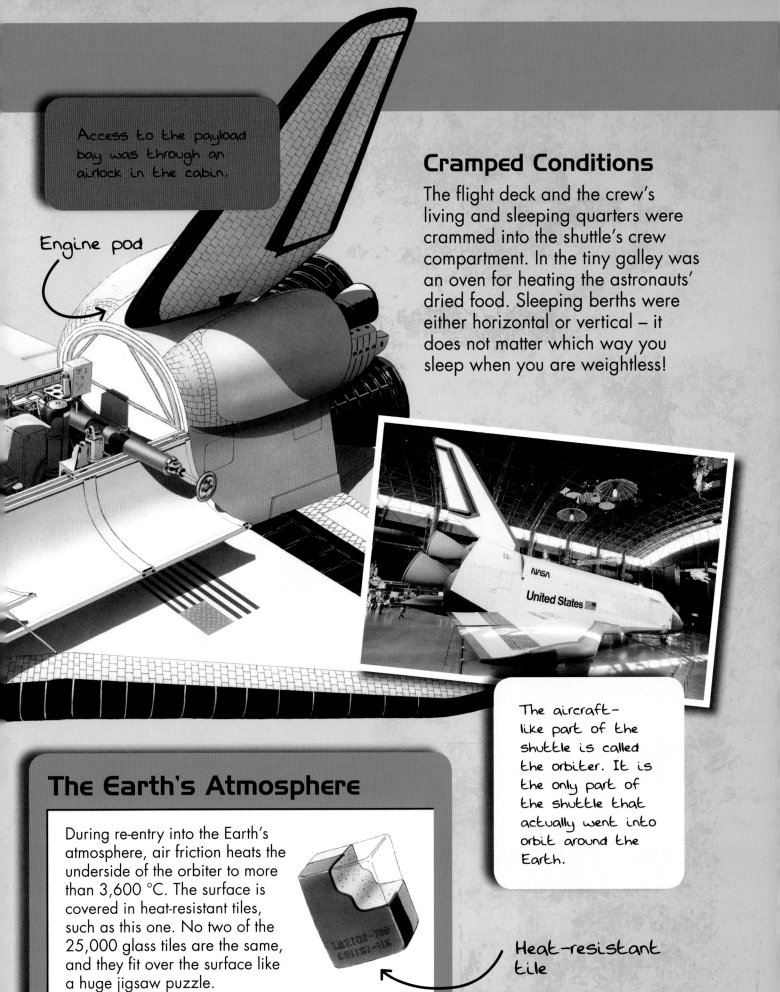

Access to the payload bay was through an airlock in the cabin.

Engine pod

Cramped Conditions

The flight deck and the crew's living and sleeping quarters were crammed into the shuttle's crew compartment. In the tiny galley was an oven for heating the astronauts' dried food. Sleeping berths were either horizontal or vertical – it does not matter which way you sleep when you are weightless!

NASA
United States

The aircraft-like part of the shuttle is called the orbiter. It is the only part of the shuttle that actually went into orbit around the Earth.

The Earth's Atmosphere

During re-entry into the Earth's atmosphere, air friction heats the underside of the orbiter to more than 3,600 °C. The surface is covered in heat-resistant tiles, such as this one. No two of the 25,000 glass tiles are the same, and they fit over the surface like a huge jigsaw puzzle.

Heat-resistant tile

25

Space Shuttle Launch

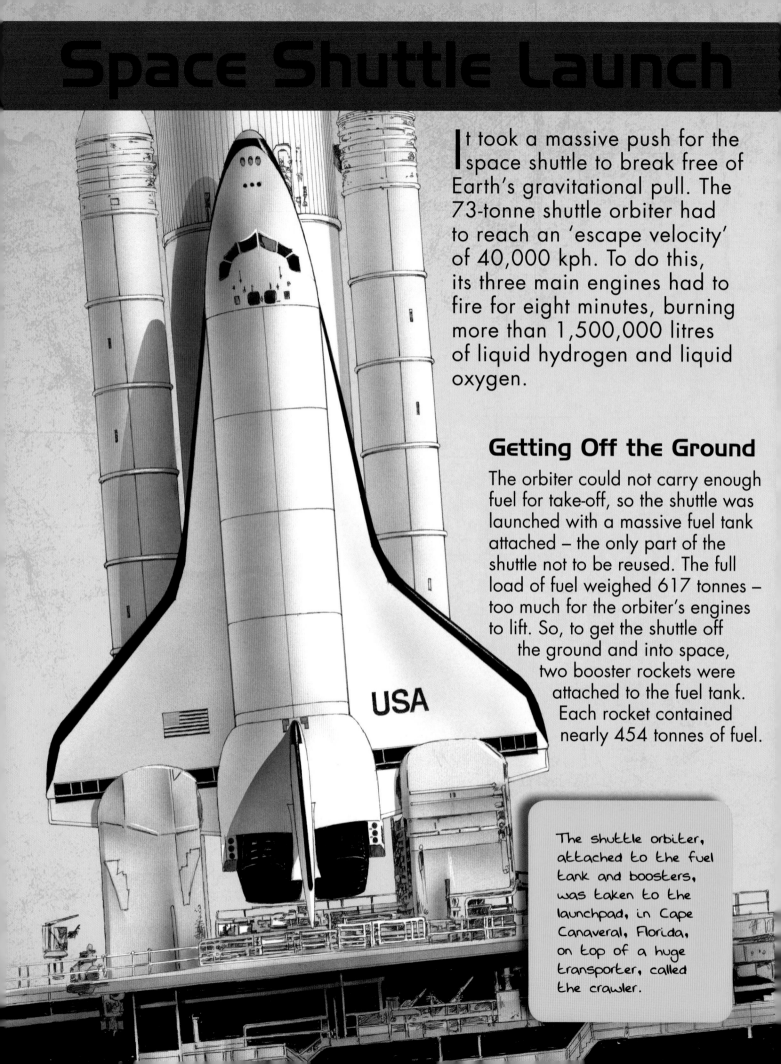

It took a massive push for the space shuttle to break free of Earth's gravitational pull. The 73-tonne shuttle orbiter had to reach an 'escape velocity' of 40,000 kph. To do this, its three main engines had to fire for eight minutes, burning more than 1,500,000 litres of liquid hydrogen and liquid oxygen.

Getting Off the Ground

The orbiter could not carry enough fuel for take-off, so the shuttle was launched with a massive fuel tank attached – the only part of the shuttle not to be reused. The full load of fuel weighed 617 tonnes – too much for the orbiter's engines to lift. So, to get the shuttle off the ground and into space, two booster rockets were attached to the fuel tank. Each rocket contained nearly 454 tonnes of fuel.

The shuttle orbiter, attached to the fuel tank and boosters, was taken to the launchpad, in Cape Canaveral, Florida, on top of a huge transporter, called the crawler.

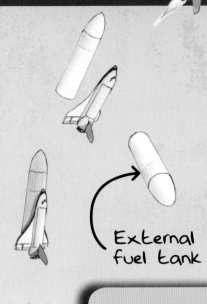

Into Orbit

Three main engines and the two boosters were fired at lift-off. Two minutes later, at an altitude of 50 km, the boosters shut down, separated and fell back to Earth. After eight minutes, at an altitude of 95 km, the main engines shut down and the fuel tank was jettisoned and burned up in the atmosphere.

External fuel tank

Small engines in the orbiter moved it into orbit, at a height of 300 km.

Astronauts control the flight of the orbiter from a two-seater cockpit that looks much like that of a jet airliner.

Booster rockets

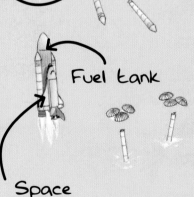

Fuel tank

Space shuttle

Back Down to the Earth

After a mission, the orbiter drops into the Earth's atmosphere, is slowed down by flying in sweeping turns and then glides onto a runway.

Incredible Facts

Well-travelled

Between its launch, in 1928, and 1937, the *Graf Zeppelin* airship made more than 500 transatlantic flights, covering more than 1.6 million km. It was also the first airship to circumnavigate the world.

Big Postbag

In an Imperial Airways flying boat there was space in the baggage and mail hold for 2 tonnes of postbags and other freight.

Heavy Going

With a full load of passengers and carrying more than 200,000 litres of aviation fuel, a Boeing 747 weighs 308 tonnes. At this weight, it needs over 3 km of runway to reach take-off speed.

Gigantic Folly

Multimillionaire Howard Hughes' seaplane *the Hughes H4 Spruce Goose* was designed to carry up to 750 passengers. It flew only once, in 1947, for less than 1 km, piloted by Hughes himself. The plane's size and weight made it impractical for regular flight.

Amazing Power

At lift-off, the five F-1 engines of *Saturn V* produced 3.4 million kg of thrust. These same engines rocketed the Apollo spacecraft 64 km above the Earth.

Captive Audience

Around 600 million people watched on live TV as Neil Armstrong stepped onto the Moon on 20 July 1969. This remained a world record until 1981, when 750 million people watched the wedding of Prince Charles and Diana Spencer.

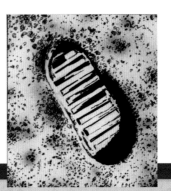

Taking the Heat

When the space shuttle re-entered the Earth's atmosphere, air friction heated the underside of the orbiter to over 3,600 °C. To resist the heat, the surface was covered in 25,000 silica glass tiles.

Slow Start

The gigantic crawler transporter that carried the space shuttle to its launchpad is the world's largest self-powered land vehicle. It is 40 m long, 35 m wide, weighs 2,858 tonnes and has a top speed of 1.6 kph.

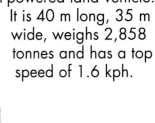

Glossary

Aluminium a metal often used for aircraft.

Ascent moving upward.

Cargo goods transported from one place to another.

Docking the joining of one vehicle with another.

Fuselage the tubular section that forms the main body of an aircraft.

Gondola a compartment that hangs beneath an airship and that may contain the control cabin, accommodation or engines.

Jettison to abandon something – for example, an empty fuel tank.

Lunar to do with the Moon.

Micro-organisms tiny living things, such as viruses and bacteria.

Military to do with the armed forces.

Orbit the path an object follows around a planet. A spacecraft is kept in orbit by its speed and the gravity of the planet.

Satellite an object that orbits a planet. The artificial satellites we send into space send information back to the Earth via radio signals.

Seismic to do with earthquakes or lunar quakes.

Streamlined designed to move easily through air or water.

Weightless the feeling of being in zero gravity, so that you float about. Astronauts in orbit feel weightless.

Index